DOWNSIZING WITHOUT DISASTER

A Thoughtful Approach To Planned Workforce Reduction

Lynn Tylczak

D1561293

CRISP PUBLICATIONS, INC.
Los Altos, California

DOWNSIZING WITHOUT DISASTER
A Thoughtful Approach to
Planned Workforce Reduction

Lynn Tylczak

CREDITS
Editor: **Nancy Shotwell**
Typesetting and Design: **Interface Studio**
Cover Design: **Carol Harris**
Artwork: **Ralph Mapson**

Copyright © 1991 by Crisp Publications, Inc.
Printed in the United States of America

Crisp books are distributed in Canada by Reid Publishing, Ltd., P.O. Box 7267, Oakville, Ontario, Canada L6J 6L6.

In Australia by Career Builders, P.O. Box 1051, Springwood, Brisbane, Queensland, Australia 4127.

And in New Zealand by Career Builders, P.O. Box 571, Manurewa, New Zealand.

Library of Congress Catalog Card Number 90-83483
Tylczak, Lynn
Downsizing Without Disaster
ISBN 1-56052-081-7

INTRODUCTION

Your company should be in such good company! The roster reads like a Who's Who of winning businesses:

Eastman Kodak, Xerox, Chevron, Du Pont, Eastern Airlines, AT&T, Oscar Mayer Food Company, Union Carbide, USX, General Motors, Exxon, IBM, Boeing, National Semiconductor, Crocker National Bank, Digital Equipment, Phillips Petroleum, Owens-Corning, Apple, Bethlehem Steel, Chrysler, Bell and Howell, BankAmerica, Salomon Brothers, United Airlines, Honeywell, Ford Motor Company, Unysis, Mobil, Wang Laboratories, Sears Roebuck and Company, to name a few.

Yet, each of these is, in a way, both a winner and a loser. We have seen their *winning* ways in such areas as market share, profitability, growth, innovation, return on investment, sales and marketing, etc. We have also seen them *lose* large numbers of employees when necessary to maintain their viability. For example:

- In the mid 1980's, Owens-Corning laid off one fifth of its employees.

- AT&T dropped from a pre-divestiture army of one million employees to less than 350,000.

- Employment levels at USX (formerly U.S. Steel) fell by 70%.

- IBM has closed several facilities (such as the Greencastle, Indiana, plant, eliminating 985 jobs in the 8400 member community) even though it maintains a "full employment" practice (e.g., no layoffs).

The above examples are typical. Fortune 500 companies have slashed 3.5 million jobs over the last ten years and it doesn't look like the trend will end.

Still, we need to be realistic rather than pessimistic. Downsizing has nothing to do with *losers* and everything to do with *losing*. Losing employees—terminating people—isn't fun. But it isn't fatal either. Downsizing is not a sign of corporate failure. It is a sign of the times.

Lynn Tylczak

PREFACE

Consider these facts:

- 30% of the firms that downsize in one year will also downsize in the next.

- 68% of all white-collar layoffs are based on seniority rather than ability or performance.

- Large firms (5000 plus employees) downsize staff by an average 6.3%, smaller firms cut by 12.6%.

- 64% of the "downsize" managers surveyed say they are expected to increase output with a decreased staff.

- Large firms are 40% more likely to downsize than smaller ones.

- 48.1% of the "downsize" managers surveyed say they have more direct reports (only 7.8% have fewer).

- Half of the "downsize" managers surveyed say they are working longer hours and are under far more stress.

- 43% of all companies cut staff as a way to "control costs."

- 36% of companies with current plans to downsize believe that they are not well prepared.

The numbers are sobering. Still, the purpose of this book isn't to argue the merits of downsizing. Downsizing, like many other managerial mandates, *simply exists*. The purpose of this self study text is to help you cope with the challenges and opportunities downsizing presents.
The objectives of this book are to:

- Probe the inherent—but avoidable—dangers of downsizing

- Profile the advantages and disadvantages of the seven most popular downsizing options

- Give you a step-by-step process to determine and fine tune your best downsizing procedures

- Help you develop implementation action plans

Forget downsizing doom and gloom. Downsizing can be a positive experience, both for corporate profits and, when properly done, for individual careers. Cutbacks offer perils *and* payoffs. Decide to treat the situation as an opportunity rather than a tragedy. Your downsizing success is up to you.

TABLE OF CONTENTS

P A R T

I

What Is Downsizing?

"I HAVE SOME NEWS FOR YOU"

WHAT IS DOWNSIZING?

Simply put, downsizing is "planned workforce reduction." It can be defined as much more. Depending on the point of view, downsizing can be: a repudiation of the unspoken employer/employee contract (do your job and you'll keep your job); a mockery of company loyalty ("I worked there 30 years!"); or as a community coffin nail (e.g. when Boeing laid off thousands of workers, King County billboards read "Will the last person leaving Seattle please turn out the lights?"). It can also be seen as an admission of managerial incompetence and corporate failure.

Translation: A Bad Thing.

Companies and managers, however, often see downsizing in a different light. It can be a chance to improve corporate flexibility and profits or an opportunity to give individuals more control and authority. It can be a method to facilitate better communications and decision-making. Or, often, as a way to redirect corporate efforts to compete effectively in a changing market.

Clarification: A Good Thing.

In the final analysis, downsizing is what *you* decide to do. The plans you make. The strategies you follow. The way you treat employees. The way you accept change. The way you help others accept it. In short, downsizing is a *management challenge*.

Summation: Downsizing is what you make it.

You can make it despite downsizing.

So decide to make it a success.

WHY DO COMPANIES DOWNSIZE?

Companies downsize for a variety of reasons. Some of the most common include:

- mergers/acquisitions/divestitures
- market shifts and loss of market share
- expensive litigation and large settlements
- plant obsolescence
- uncollectable accounts
- changes in technology
- increased competition
- loss of major customer or supplier
- desire for increased worker flexibility
- unacceptable profits or profit margins
- loss of financing/drop in bond ratings/loss of industry credit
- expired or challenged patents
- change in organizational structure or procedures
- drop in exchange rates
- recession
- lagging productivity
- trade deficit
- absorption of "baby boom"
- changes in government regulation (i.e., deregulation)
- unacceptable administrative or overhead costs

There are many reasons for companies to downsize. Since virtually any of these conditions can happen at any time, you should be prepared.

REPLACE FEAR WITH FACTS

Downsizing is not a simple, clear cut procedure. Both managers and employees have feelings. Most managers who are called upon to do it hate downsizing. As a result, downsizing is often as much of a *problem* as it is a *solution*.

Downsizing creates fear within management. There is fear because of uncertainty:

- How will downsizing affect the company? Affect my subordinates? Affect me?

- Will I lose my job too?

- I was trained to deal with growth, not downsizing. Can I survive the process?

It's possible, however, to replace fear with facts. Companies survive downsizing. Managers survive downsizing. Both can profit from it. The difference between those who succeed and those who recede is *planning and attitude*. This difference is expanded in the strategies and procedures outlined in the rest of this book.

P A R T

II

Seven
Downsizing Issues

EENIE
MEENIE
MYNIE
MOE

SEVEN DOWNSIZING ISSUES

The road to downsizing has more potholes than an unrepaired road. Everywhere you turn, another problem threatens to blow the plan. Employee morale snaps like a whiplash victim. Managerial control and cost estimates get a serious jolt. It is often a very bumpy ride.

Before you downsize, it is essential to prepare some "future shock" absorbers. There are seven common downsizing problems/issues.

THE SEVEN PROBLEMS/ISSUES

Issue #1: The Ego Blow

Issue #2: Crowd Control

Issue #3: All For None and None For All

Issue #4: Beware the Backlash

Issue #5: Reducing the Workload

Issue #6: Downsizing Syndrome

Issue #7: Controlling Interest

Recognize and deal with each and you won't be stopped dead in your tracks. The key to successful downsizing is to keep the following in mind as you deal with these issues.

1. Analyze potential problems.

2. Communicate the problems to those affected.

3. Map out the appropriate action.

4. Communicate the action plan to those affected.

5. HAVE THE COMMITMENT TO MAKE IT WORK.

ISSUE #1
THE EGO BLOW

ANALYSIS

''I remember my first downsizing like it was yesterday,'' says the Production Supervisor of a large silicon chip manufacturer. ''Top management told me to cut the line by 10%. I thought 'You don't just 'cut a line,' you terminate—*fire!*—people. Mothers and fathers. Teammates on the bowling team. Friends I eat lunch with. Kids I hired off the street. People who work hard and deserve better'.''

Downsizing is a trying and often humiliating experience for managers *and* employees. When you lay a person off, he/she receives two messages:

1. We don't need you here anymore (we may wish we did, but that changes nothing).

2. We don't want you here anymore (mostly because we don't need you, but again that changes nothing).

That is a very painful message to get. It is also a painful message to give. The result often is that morale drops to rock bottom. Productivity goes downhill. Workers and ex-workers may strike back at the company. The financial bottom line can drop even lower.

THE PROBLEM

People have feelings. Your challenge is knowing how to minimize (and if possible, circumvent) the bad ones.

ISSUE #2
CROWD CONTROL

ANALYSIS

Downsizing affects many different constituencies. The affectations of any one can easily double your downsizing difficulties.

Consider the MIA's—those Men and Women Influenced by the Action:

- Managers
- Laid-off employees
- "Survivors" (those employees who retain jobs with the company)
- Minority workers
- Customers
- Competitors
- Suppliers
- Local community
- Media
- Shareholders

Each group receives something different out of a downsizing experience. Members of the terminated team take their knocks and severance pay. Survivors take a guilt trip ("Why not me?"). Competitors try to take your business away from concerned customers. Suppliers take special precautions with your corporate line of credit. The media may take the story and give you more publicity than you ever thought (or hoped) was possible. The community also gets in the act.

THE PROBLEM

Downsizing requires managers to *simultaneously* deal with these different constituents. You need a plan if you plan to survive.

12

ISSUE #3
ALL FOR NONE AND NONE FOR ALL

ANALYSIS

The most stressful downsizing decision is also the most basic: who stays and who goes?

Consider the options. You can:

- terminate employees based on seniority
- terminate employees based on their skill/productivity level
- terminate a set percentage of employees in every department
- terminate an entire department and anybody unlucky enough to be in it
- terminate employees based on average department growth
- terminate an entire job level or position (e.g., second line managers)

Each option assigns personnel to a different personal category. When you create categories—when you differentiate workers—you can unintentionally divide one corporation into two teams: us vs. them.*

These "categorical" options can both ingratiate and aggravate. For example, a decision to use seniority levels as the basis for layoffs will be sanctified by the old guard and vilified by the new.

THE PROBLEM

A number of employees have to go. This changes the basic chemistry of the corporate. The corporate creed changes from "all for one and one for all" to "all for one—and that one is ME!" A person looking out for himself or herself isn't looking out for the best interests of the company.

---

*NOTE: The "two team" premise has many possible permutations. Those with seniority vs. those without. Department A people vs. the Bs and beyond. Hard workers vs. the hardly working. The perspectives vary with team definitions. Things get *really* complicated when teams overlap (hard working people with seniority who are in Department A vs....).

ISSUE #4
BEWARE THE BACKLASH

Downsizing Without Disaster

ANALYSIS

Let's say you've already dealt with Issue #3. On a personal level, you think you've identified Who Has To Go. Before you go any further, think of the potential business backlash. For example:

- Terminating employees based on seniority

  Major problems:

  Losing younger workers with newer, more critical computer/technological skills.
  This approach may also gut the company's Affirmative Action Plan.
  It will certainly complicate future recruitment.

- Terminating employees based on their skill or productivity level

  Major problems:

  Identifying who the best workers truly are.
  Preparing adequate individual documentation (would it stand up in court?).
  The ability to evaluate the qualitative as well as the quantitative.

- Terminating a set percentage of employees in every department

  Major problems:

  Punishing efficient departments.
  May not produce the necessary savings (managers tend to lay off the lowest, rather than average-wage workers).
  May not address future corporate needs.

- Terminating an entire department and anybody unlucky enough to be in it

  Major problems:

  Accidentally terminating an ''ugly duckling department.''
  Decisions are sometimes based on popularity, not profitability.
  Great workers may be caught in the wrong place at the wrong time.

- Terminating employees based on above average department growth

  Major problems:

  Comparing apples and oranges. Example: total staff doubled, the personnel staff tripled. Cut personnel people? No. Not when new EEO, cafeteria benefits, drug/alcohol testing, etc., programs quadrupled staff workload. Fastest growing staff levels often reflect productivity or opportunity for future growth. Perhaps the fastest growing department is also the company's fastest growing profit center!

ISSUE #4
BEWARE THE BACKLASH (Continued)

• Terminating an entire job level (e.g., second line managers)

Major problems:

Terminating staff—without terminating the related tasks/responsibilities/authority. Who's going to do the work?.

Losing the recruitment base for promotions, retiree replacements, etc.

Overstressing managers (if you eliminate all second line managers, you probably treble the span of control of the next management level).

THE PROBLEM

It is difficult to know which short term action will hurt the least in the long term. Often, managers must guess which cut will leave the smallest scar.

ISSUE #5
REDUCING THE WORKLOAD

ANALYSIS

It's a curious and common paradox: downsize the staff, upsize the workload.

Example: ten employees run the Credit and Collection Department. The staff is reduced by two people. The duties, responsibilities, concerns, workload, etc., of the canned colleagues are divided among the remaining eight. Since the department was already overworked, morale plummets. Three of the remaining eight workers soon quit. They are not easily replaced (would you go to work for a company that just axed a position just like the one you were applying for?). The work piles up. Quality suffers.

In layoff lingo, these eight employees are called ''survivors.'' More precisely, they are the walking wounded.

Reconsider this Credit and Collection catastrophe. A few changes might have downsized the workload without downsizing profitability or practicality. Ask:

- Are all C&C reports necessary? Could any be eliminated? Trimmed? Simplified? Automated? Produced less frequently? Distributed to fewer people? Done more easily by others?

- Would quality suffer if the staff checked fewer credit references? Made fewer crosschecks? Did fewer followups?

- Could general tasks be reassigned? Could the responsibility for C&C form letters be transferred to the typing pool? Could outstanding balances be assigned to a collection agency when they are 120, rather than 180, days past due?

When you downsize staff, you have to downsize the workload.

THE PROBLEM

Downsizing the workload requires as much analysis and attention as downsizing the staff. Few managers know where to begin.

ISSUE #6
DOWNSIZING SYNDROME

ANALYSIS

Defective downsizing can kill the organization it was trying to save. The corporate structure—the skeleton—may survive, but the company loses muscle and, on occasion, its heart and soul.

Consider these categories:

- **LOYALTY.** Company loyalty is replaced with a personal pledge: ''If the company can't take care of me, I'll take care of myself.''

- **JOB SECURITY.** Security evaporates. People don't think about surviving the last round of layoffs. They worry about the next time around. They spend their time playing politics and covering their backsides.

- **INITIATIVE.** Initiative and creativity all but disappear. They involve risk. Most people lay low during and after major layoffs.

- **HUMANITY.** When the basic problem is money, people become a ''cost item.'' Companies pay dearly for this kind of insensitivity.

- **PERSPECTIVE.** After a downsizing, managers focus on quantitative concerns (systems, structure, strategy) and ignore qualitative concepts (staff, style, skills, shared values). All are important for a well-balanced business.

- **INSPIRATION.** Early retirement programs can deprive the company of mentors and leaders. Departmental cutbacks may starve exciting projects/products.

- **AMBITION.** When a company eliminates management layers, once ambitious managers find themselves in a career cul-de-sac.

When a company loses in these categories, it loses its future.

THE PROBLEM

Downsizing changes the corporate culture. How can we make sure these changes are for the good?

ISSUE #7
CONTROLLING INTEREST

ANALYSIS

Companies downsize as a response. Often, this response is to a loss of control over the business. Downsizing is a reaction to a strong business stimulus (see Why Companies Downsize). When managers can't control the outside business environment, they try to control their internal expenses. Payroll is usually the biggest ticket item. Is it any wonder that so many employees get a one way ticket out?

Paradoxically, downsizing can often cause businesses to lose—rather than gain—all kinds of control. Consider these cases:

Cost Control

Cut costs? In the first quarter of 1985. Du Pont spent $125 million on downsizing because of severance pay, early retirement incentives, etc. It hardly sounds like cost control.

According to *Management Review*, the payback period for direct downsizing costs alone runs between 12 and 16 months. Add indirect costs (lost training/development, eventual recruitment/replacement, low productivity, increased turnover, etc.) and the cost benefits of downsizing are often not felt for months or even years.

Productivity Control

In 1987, employees at Bell and Howell heard layoff rumors. They spent less time working and more time separating the wheat from the chaff at the old rumor mill. Productivity plummeted, corporate profits fell by 11%.

Workforce Control

Bethlehem Steel cut its workforce from 89,000 to 33,400. Pre-downsizing, only a few salaried workers were unionized (and these were all at a single plant). Post-downsizing, the union signed up 700 new salaried employees company wide.

ISSUE #7
CONTROLLING INTEREST (Continued)

Staffing Control

Du Pont hoped that its open-ended voluntary retirement program would cut 6500 employees. Twice that many left. Four hundred were asked to delay their departure until replacements could be identified and trained.

That's not unusual. Voluntary separation policies often will attract 50–100% more employees than desired. A significant percentage of those leaving are employees that the company specifically wants to keep.

THE PROBLEM

A company downsizes to gain additional control over specific aspects of its business. For every "X" of control it gains in said areas, it stands to lose "5X" worth of control over unspoken issues.

SUMMARY

Downsizing is riddled with problems. But despite all you have read so far, there are solutions.

Downsizing problems can be modified, solved and/or circumvented, if you:

- Recognize potential problems
- Communicate downsizing problems openly with all affected
- Map appropriate action plans
- Involve those affected persons in the plans
- Implement said plans effectively
- Respond to honest feedback

P A R T

III

Planning

THE BEST LAID PLANS

Downsizing requires a four point plan:

1. Strategic Planning

Up front analysis is critical. Many companies, fearing analysis paralysis, do not invest the time necessary to consider where they are and where they need to be. This is false economy. Instead of making a plan that accomplishes their stated objectives, they react with a series of hastily prepared decisions.

Replace "ready, aim, fire" with "ready, fire, aim" and you're likely to end up with "ready, fire...thud."

2. Program Planning

Thanks to strategic planning, you should know where you are and where you need to be. Program planning is a detailed map to get you from here to there. It identifies the who, what, when, why, and how of what needs to happen.

3. Implementation

This is where it all comes together—assuming you did a solid job on steps 1 and 2—or all comes apart. This step has all the pain and most of the gain.

4. Follow-Up

Follow-up involves two processes: evaluation (how did we do?) and prevention (how can we avoid having to go through this again?).

STRATEGIC PLANNING*

Asking who/what the company is and who/what it wants to be isn't existential. It's essential. Business is a journey. You can't plan a successful trip without knowing your point of origin and your destination. Without planning, you can—and will—get lost.

Start slowly. Even the longest journey begins with a single step—deciding where you are.

STEP 1—WHERE YOU ARE

Conduct a thorough inventory of your business condition. Take your time. In fact, take as much time as you can afford (time often being a limited commodity in a downsizing market).

Analyze such issues as:

- Current problems/opportunities and their nature
- Current staffing levels/costs and their relation to revenues/profits
- Staff strengths and weaknesses
- Competitive position and how downsizing could affect it
- Strategic issues (corporate goals, plans, objectives, missions, philosophies, etc.)
- Organizational structure (levels of staff support, span of control, etc.)
- Redundancies (in production, management, reporting, etc.)
- Management responsibilities, authority, accountability
- Current value judgments (e.g. centralized authority is ''better'')
- Business weaknesses and strengths (including such issues as market share, plant obsolescence, high training costs, expiring/emerging patents, etc.)
- The acid tests: if you were buying this business, what would you want to know about it? How would you change it?

Consider your current corporation carefully. Don't be surprised if you find people and programs adding clutter rather than value.

---

* Ironically, given the proper preliminary analysis, you may find that downsizing isn't the answer after all. It might be reorganizing. In this text, however, we will accept the decision to downsize at face value.

Where You Are—An Example

Let's say managerial span of control is an important issue in your business because competitors have lower overhead. You need to determine the need for overseeing a project. Different corporate cultures require different amounts of supervision. For example, some circumstances require less circumspect management:

	Requires Minimal Supervision	Requires Extensive Supervision
subordinate tasks are varied and complex		X
subordinate tasks are routine and similar	X	
subordinates are interdependent	X	
subordinates have strong work ethic, loyalty, maturity, commitment, trust, attitude about quality	X	
planning/direction/control are required		X
complex inner and inter department relations		X
close geographic proximity	X	
heterogeneous staff	X	
formal organization		X
substantial staff/MIS support	X	
wide skill mix	X	
autonomous subordinates	X	

THINK IT THROUGH!

STRATEGIC PLANNING (Continued)

STEP 2—WHERE YOU WANT TO BE

Deciding where you want your organization to stand in the future is not a stand alone concept. Where you will stand in the future will also depend on where you stood in the past.

As a result, step 2 is basically an extension of step 1. You use Form A on the facing page to:

- Separate each point identified in step 1

- Note where you would like to see changes/improvements made

- Develop/state future goals/objectives

Sounds easy, doesn't it? But step 2 requires as much introspection and direction as step 1. For example:

- Goals and objectives should allow a company to stretch without leaving stretchmarks.

- Don't oversimplify. "Solve the problem" may be too simplistic a goal to be realistic. Perhaps a more tractable tact would be to circumvent the problem, lessen its impact, manipulate it into an opportunity, etc.

Where You Want to Be—An Example

Your overhead may turn out to be an opportunity. Have you ever considered selling the overhead functions in your organization the way you sell your other products? Control Data has made a business out of contracting out personnel functions; Xerox sells logistics and distribution services; Parsons Princkerhoff sells public relations help, and IBM has an entire profit center devoted to leasing. Why couldn't you do something equally creative?

STRATEGIC PLANNING

FORM A

NOTE: There is no right response to the "where do we go from here" question. There is only the answer you think best for your company.

Consider how three different managers using this form could respond to the same point.

POINT #	WHERE WE STAND	NEEDS CHANGE	WHERE WE WANT TO STAND
1	Overhead is 5% higher than competitor's overhead	X	Manager of the ABC Company says: We want to cut overhead by 5%—if they can do it so can we!
1	Overhead is 5% higher than competitor's overhead	X	Manager of the XYZ Company says: No change—our overhead is higher because we provide more customer service—it is our major competitive advantage.
1	Overhead is 5% higher than competitor's overhead.	X	Manager of the Alphabet Ltd. says: We want to cut overhead by 7%—we offer similar support to competitors and should do better because of our MIS.

PROGRAM PLANNING

Strategic planning has given us the "wheres": where we are and where we want to be. Program planning completes our queries by answering the whos, whats, whens, whys and hows.

WHEN?

This is a two-part problem.

- When do we let workers go?

- When must we/should we/do we let workers know?

  The "must we" is potentially a function of legislative mandate. For example, the Workers Adjustment and Retraining Notification (WARN) Act provides that, with certain exceptions, employers of 100 or more workers must give at least 60 days' advance notice of a plant closing or mass layoff to affected workers or their representatives, to the State dislocated worker unit, and to the appropriate local government.

  The "should we" assumes that you have more lead time than mandated.

  The "do we" is what we focus on. Assuming we have choices, when do we choose to announce the downsizing?

WHAT?

What downsizing options are available? One-size-fits-all options are easy to put on, while customer programs tailor the workforce to specific needs. Which provides the best corporate fit?

HOW?

How do you identify the most appropriate downsizing options for your organization? Each alternative has pros and cons. You must decide which approach has the best payoff.

WHO?

Who receives outplacement assistance? Is a universal plan outside budgetary limits?

WHY?

Why did "X" employees lose their jobs? Why cut "X" number of dollars? Why not "X+1"? Or "X-1"? Or some other number?

Who, what, when, where, why. It's how we develop a strong program plan.

PROGRAM PLANNING—WHEN?

THE FIRST TIME ISSUE: When to let workers go

Most companies lay excess employees off ASAP—As Soon As Practical. Layoffs may wait until a particular project is finished, until other planning steps are completed, until the end of the pay period/month, or until downsizing details meet statutory (e.g., WARN)/union requirements. Practical is tactical.

It's also smart to act ASAP because many companies procrastinate on pare downs. Time is money—yet they spend every possible minute avoiding the inevitable. Companies are only human.

PROGRAM PLANNING—WHEN? (Continued)

THE SECOND TIME ISSUE: When to let workers know

In a Utopian world, workers would have plenty of advance notice. However, in the real world, it may not be possible or desirable to give a longer-than-mandated lead time.

The advantages/disadvantages of a more-than-mandated advance notice:

+ Workers think you are giving them an advantage, not taking one. They have additional time to prepare for their pink slip, to find new jobs and accept the inevitable. This can slash unemployment and outplacement costs.

+ Play by the golden rules. Employees are asked to give at least two week's notice, despite a lack of laws. Shouldn't you be up front as well?

+ The company presents a better image. Downsizing is not a spur of the moment, let's dock-the-dockworkers kind of thing. It is spurred by serious business backslides. Prove that you run the company without running out on employees

+ Pros and Cons Paradox Part 1: Survivors may feel less guilt ("They knew it was coming...")

− Short tempered short timers may sabotage, bad mouth, or embarass the company and surviving staff.

− Additional advance notice advances employees plan. Workers may leave earlier than anticipated and leave projects in the lurch.

− Breaking the news as close as possible to a layoff helps the company (though perhaps not the employees) make a clean break.

− Dam the cash flow. Now. Every day means more wages to pay.

− Pros and Cons Paradox Part II: Survivors may feel more guilt ("Whenever I see Frank I think about...")

The question is: When do you tell employees? The answer is: it depends on your corporate culture (and, of course, the law!). Some companies think their employees need protection from the outside world. Others think they need protection from their employees. Most would sum up the situation in less drastic terms.

You need to ask:

- Do workers know that the company is in trouble?

- Will it be easy for them to find new jobs?

- Will they resent the company or the situation?

- Does the company appear to be downsizing because it needs to or because it wants to?

- Were other cost-conscious measures taken before jobs?

- Could employees interpret the downsizing as a punitive program?

- Are managers immune to staff cuts?

In short, it's a moral issue: given the corporate conditions, what would people consider an indecent advance?

Know your employees and you'll know the appropriate timetable.

PROGRAM PLANNING—WHAT?

No matter what downsizing option(s) you choose, you are going to upset people. That's the nature of the problem.

The most popular downsizing options are:

- Terminating employees based on seniority:

    Option #1—Last hired, first fired

    Option #2—Offer an early retirement program

- Terminating employees based on their skill or productivity level

- Terminating a set percentage of employees in every department

- Terminating an entire department and anybody unlucky enough to be in it

- Terminating employees based on above average department growth

- Terminating an entire job level/position

What option will work best in your business? Study the pros and cons carefully. They will be the basis for your decision.

OPTION #1—Terminating employees based on seniority— Last hired, first fired

THE PROS

- easy to administer
- easy to justify
- relatively low cost (newer employees have lower salaries, therefore lower unemployment, severance, etc., costs)
- politically practical (old timers have more clout)
- less guilt (new—translation: younger—employees may have an easier time getting a new job, relocating, training, etc.)
- rewards loyalty (they stuck with you, you stick by them)
- legally defensible
- endorsed by most unions

THE CONS

- does not address the future needs and cultural changes of the company (you *need* people with more current technological skills, varied backgrounds, etc.; long term employees may have more trouble adapting to change)
- makes future recruiting more difficult
- tends to fall hardest on minorities/women
- does not address the value of specific employees, skills, or positions
- company may have to replace workers who had critical skills (leading to the inevitable question: ''Why did you lay them off in the first place?'')
- difficulty in meeting budgetary needs (layoffs will be relatively large because new hires have below average salaries)
- certain departments will be hit harder than others (some traditionally have a high percentage of new hires)
- high cost workers/managers may be forced to do low value work

WHAT? PROS & CONS (Continued)

> ## OPTION #2—Terminating employees based on seniority— early retirement program

THE PROS

- significant long term savings
- employees have margin of control (''Yes, I'd like to retire'')
- high wage workers most likely targets
- positive company image
- little stress
- little guilt
- little panic
- opens promotional opportunities for survivors
- opportunity to bring fresh thinkers into important positions

THE CONS

- lose important people that you need
- release retirees young enough to join competitors, start personal businesses (taking some of your good employees with them!), etc.
- survivors lose mentors/direction/leadership
- less management control (employee choice means less management voice)
- high up-front costs
- may need to loosen or change retirement requirements so that enough people qualify
- leaving voluntarily may give the impression of ''get out while the getting is good''
- too many people may opt out
- if too few choose retirement, you may have to sweeten the pot (problem: how will this play with first round retirees?)
- if too few choose retirement, corporate pressures (but not the ''pot'') may increase

OPTION #3—Terminating employees based on their skill or productivity level

THE PROS

- you can retain the best workers
- you reward past achievements
- you provide positive feedback for future performance
- you get rid of ''deadwood''
- increases employee morale (good workers no longer have to carry the weight of poor performers)
- you can layoff troublesome workers (those with high absentee or tardy rates, discipline or attitude problems, etc.)
- addresses company needs
- separates workers from extraneous issues (current positions, age, time on the job, etc.)

THE CONS

- difficult to define the critical measurements (their application should be constant companywide)
- difficult to identify the best workers
- individual productivity may have been affected by peripheral problems (old equipment, lack of materials, poor supervision, etc.) that might change under the new order
- difficult to justify to individuals
- difficult to document decisions (they might be challenged in court)

WHAT? PROS & CONS (Continued)

OPTION #4—Terminating a set percentage of employees in every department

THE PROS

- easy to administer
- appears "fair" (every department takes an equal hit)
- department managers maintain staff control (they know which employees they need to keep)
- easy to justify
- no level is immune to layoffs (managers lose jobs in departments with a dense management/professional population)
- non political—the focus is on layoffs, not specific departments
- does not impact on department balance, power, importance, etc.

THE CONS

- punishes efficient departments
- may not produce necessary savings (managers lay off new hires with below average salaries)
- does not address corporate needs
- does not address departmental needs
- cuts in some departments will have a disproportionate impact on other departments (a small cut in personnel—laying off the switchboard operator— would seriously impact the efficiency of the sales, credit, customer service, etc., departments)
- does not recognize the relative value of specific departments
- does not recognize the relative value of employees
- same difficulty in selecting who is to be laid off
- departments that require extensive/expensive training are most adversely affected

OPTION #5—Terminating an entire department and anybody unlucky enough to be in it

THE PROS

- easy to administer
- little guilt (survivors outside the department don't know the victims personally)
- in business, it's often better to kill than cripple
- provides a clean break
- predictable savings
- hits at all levels (managers, professionals, support staff)
- the cut may be "invisible" (particularly if the unit being terminated is a separate facility)

THE CONS

- you might terminate a department that makes major non-quantitative contributions
- decision could be made on popularity, not profitability or productivity
- leaves no foundation to rebuild the department in the future
- you lose workers through no fault of their own (particularly troublesome if they were winners transferred to this department as troubleshooters)
- complete loss of experience/expertise/support/input/investment
- fixed costs/tasks may remain (security/maintenance/property taxes on a closed facility don't go away)
- the loss may be very visible

WHAT? PROS & CONS (Continued)

OPTION #6—Terminating employees based on above average department head count growth

THE PROS

- easy to administer
- seems fair (why should one department—particularly a support section—grow out of proportion to the others?)
- nonpolitical
- regains corporate balance
- blame falls to the department ("the department was out of control") targeted approach

THE CONS

- you may be comparing apples and oranges (if the mandated workload tripled, why shouldn't the staff double?)
- redefines the company vis a vis the department
- does not address corporate or departmental needs
- difficult to choose a timeline for growth comparison (a two-year-old MIS department will probably show disproportionate growth when compared to an old production line)
- the growth of other costs/savings needs to be considered (Department A may be investing heavily in machinery while Department B invests in people)
- difficult to predict savings

OPTION #7—Terminating an entire job level/position

(Added twist: If you know long in advance that certain jobs will be phased out, you can phase in training for those affected, giving them a chance to train for positions that the company anticipates will grow in the future.)

THE PROS

- easy to administer
- easy to identify those affected
- easy to justify ("We simply don't need that job done anymore")
- savings are easy to estimate
- no recruiting costs (when good times return, these jobs won't)
- legally defensible
- addresses needs of the company

If you accept the above, add these additional pluses:

- employees have margin of control ("Yes, I'd like to train for another position so that I can stay with the company")
- little panic
- opens promotional/growth opportunities for those most affected
- you can retain the best workers
- you get rid of "deadwood" (e.g., they won't be willing to train for other positions)
- increases morale ("My job may be leaving, but I'm not!")
- seems fair

WHAT? PROS & CONS (Continued)

OPTION #7—Terminating an entire job level/position (Continued)

THE CONS

- it may be nearly impossible to identify a truly unnecessary job

- tasks probably have to be reassigned—leading to a downsized staff with an upsized workload

- increased span of control (get rid of a level of management and the next level may treble its span of control)

- survivors may lose mentors and leadership

- does not identify the best workers

- does not recognize the relative value of an employee

- leaves no foundation to rebuild the department in the future

If you accept the above, subtract these additional negatives:

- requires a very long lead time—often THE major problem in downsizing

- requires a major commitment to training (time, money, resources, planning, etc.)

- requires the company to try to predict where jobs will be in the future

- high training costs

- workers may mistake guidance for guarantees (workers can train for *anticipated* jobs, but you can't guarantee that said jobs will be there in the future)

- workers must have the willingness—and ability—to train for other positions

- the company must be willing to pass sensitive information (e.g., strategic planning) on to employees

PLANNING PROGRAM—HOW?

RANKING THE RAMIFICATIONS

Ranking the pros and cons of each option is how many companies decide on a downsizing device.

The following form can help. *Use one copy of this form for each downsizing option.* Rate the importance of each pro and con on a scale of 1 to 10 (1—not important, 10—very important).

Add the pro points together to get Subtotal #1. Add the con column points together to get Subtotal #2. Subtract Subtotal #2 from Subtotal #1. This is your Grand Total. The higher the number, the more appropriate the option.

OPTION #1 _____

IMPORTANCE

THE PROS
    Point #1   _____
    Point #2   _____
    Point #3 etc.   _____

PROS UNIQUE TO YOUR BUSINESS*
    Point #1   _____
    Point #2   _____   **SUBTOTAL #1**

                                             _____

THE CONS
    Point #1   _____
    Point #2   _____
    Point #3 etc.   _____

CONS UNIQUE TO YOUR BUSINESS*
    Point #1   _____
    Point #2   _____   **SUBTOTAL #2**

                                              _____

    GRAND TOTAL **(Subtotal #1 minus Subtotal #2)**   _____

                                                  _____

---

*Points unique to your business might include:

- a union contract that requires renegotiation before you can pursue a specific downsizing option
- required levels of EEO or Affirmative Action personnel to retain a government contract
- an ESOP which makes it more difficult to lay off specific owner-workers
- how the number of employees you are going to lose will interface with federal mandates/union agreements. For example, if you downsize a certain number of people, your downsizing and/or reorganizing may be defined as a ''closing,'' which has entirely different legal ramifications. Talk to a lawyer who specializes in layoff legalities!

PLANNING PROGRAM—WHO?

Outplacement services often are used to smooth the process of downsizing. Outgoing offerings, once thought to be paternalistic (we'll take care of you), are now recognized as realistic (we'll take care of ourselves—placement programs help avoid age discrimination and fair employment practice lawsuits, survivor stress and guilt, etc.). No wonder the outplacement industry has grown approximately 40% a year since 1980.

Unfortunately, when you downsize employees, you often see "upsized" expenses. So the common downsizing query isn't "What outplacement services should we offer," but "Who should we offer them to," and "Who will provide said services?"

WHO ARE WE OFFERING?

Outplacement services can be internally sought, externally bought, or the government lot. Consider the advantages and disadvantages of each approach:

- **Government lot**

  Many people believe that if employees need simple direction rather than complex introspection, government assistance is the appropriate offering. While it's true that government agencies can provide basic assistance and temporary compensation, they can do even better than that.

  Thanks to such legislation as the Job Training Partnership Act, the Vocational Education Act of 1984, Economically Dislocated Workers Adjustment Act (EDWAA), etc., extensive services are available. Contact your state unemployment office or the National Alliance of Business (1015 15th St., N.W., Washington, D.C., 20005, (202) 298-2900) for additional information.

- **Internally sought**

  Internal programs (usually run by the personnel or HR department) are convenient, inexpensive and available. Unfortunately, they also have drawbacks. Personnel departments may not have the expertise or desire to handle much more than a low level, routine repertoire of services (gathering/placing employment ads, typing resumés, etc.). The personnel department will be busy keeping morale and communication levels high, determining severance levels, documenting individual employee actions, etc. This may not be the time to add on yet another responsibility.

- **Externally bought**

  Excellent outplacement firms offer standout advantages, including: specialized services, experience/expertise, contacts, objectivity, good facilities, a counseling thrust, credibility, etc. Programs can be bought as a package or piecemeal.

  Major disadvantage: Cost. Group sessions can cost from $1500 per day to $4500 for a three day workshop. More specialized job search programs are even more expensive (e.g., around $750 per employee for administrative fees plus a percentage of his/her annual wage—12–15% for managers, 18–12% for top managers).

You need to ask yourself these questions:

- What kind of help do my employees need?

- What kind of help can I afford to give them?

- If I can't offer a universal outplacement plan, can I ration services so that they get to the right people? How?

- How can these services be conducted (e.g., via federal and state EDWAA funding)?

PLANNING PROGRAM—WHO? (Continued)

WHO SHOULD WE OFFER IT TO?

Outplacement assistance is like fire insurance. Everybody wants to have it—even if they never have to use it. Still, you can't underwrite everyone.

Money is usually tight when a company contracts. So outplacement program parameters should be set based on your answers to these two questions:

1. Should we offer outplacement services to exempts, non-exempts, or all ex-employees?

    Offer help only to those who need it. Managers in your industry may be a dime a dozen while skilled workers are a priceless commodity. Workers may come cheap while managers come dear. Only you know the specifics of your industry and who specifically will need the most help. Remember, if you offer assistance to *anyone* you'll have to offer less assistance to *everyone*. Don't rob "penniless Peter" to pay "full pockets Paul".

2. Who should get what services?

    Exempt employees usually require a more savvy specimen of assistance (career counselling, personal assessment, salary negotiations, role playing, etc.). Non-exempt groups tend to receive collective help (group sessions that include how to write a resumé, handle a job interview, fill out unemployment claim forms, etc.). Certain internal services (resumé typing, for example) are helpful to all.

Outplacement. Look into it, but look out for it. You don't want to buy too little or pay too much.

PROGRAM PLANNING—WHY?

There's one thing you can count on in downsizing: you have to play the numbers game. It's not a lot of fun. Nobody wants to be the #1 downsizer. The only thing worse than having to play the game is losing it.

In this numbers game, you're dealing with negative numbers. How many people will you need to lay off? How much money are you trying to save? Even the most objective numbers will be objectionable.

So take a positive posture. Don't "downsize." RIGHTSIZE. You'll find the right layoff level by questioning two quantities: budgetary needs and staffing needs. Study them separately, then coordinate for the ultimate answer.

PLANNING PROGRAM—WHY? (Continued)

STAFFING LEVEL—How many employees will you need to lay off?

This is really a two part question:

- How many employees will you need to lay off?
- How many employees can you afford to lay off?

For help, ask yourself, "Can/should I..."

	NO	YES	If yes, Number/Names of Extraneous Employees*
Close a particular division/department/section/plant	___	___	_____
Replace permanent workers with temps as needed	___	___	_____
Replace permanent workers with overtime as needed	___	___	_____
Replace permanent workers with contract employees	___	___	_____
Replace production people with manufactured materials from outside suppliers	___	___	_____
Lease/rent out employees	___	___	_____
Lower overall production levels	___	___	_____
Lower service levels	___	___	_____
Decrease the support services to line employee ratio	___	___	_____
Combine positions (for example, two bosses per secretary)	___	___	_____
Eliminate positions (for example, bosses use typing pool/clerks rather than secretaries or personal assistants)	___	___	_____
Restructure jobs/tasks	___	___	_____
Restructure the organization (e.g., eliminate levels of management)	___	___	_____
Redefine success (e.g., no payoff to bosses based on number of subordinates)	___	___	_____

*The names of these "extraneous employees" should be listed on an attached page

BUDGETARY LEVELS: How much money are you trying to save?

It's difficult to determine the appropriate amount to surmount. It will depend on the basis and biases you use for budgeting.

This direct approach will direct your efforts. Which figure/explanation pair makes the most dollars and sense?

"We want to save _____ dollars through downsizing because—"

- we have a specific need for that amount of cash (for example, the company needs to raise this much to make its quarterly debt payment)

- this amount of savings is mandated (via a merger, divestiture, acquisition, finance contract, venture capital agreement, etc.)

- this will cover losses incurred over the last (insert a specific period of time)

- top management estimates that there's that much personnel fat clogging the corporate arteries

- we want to spend the same amount/percentage on overhead as our competition

- that will put overhead expenses in line with underpinning revenues

- the stockholders (or Wall Street) demand we cut overhead dramatically— downsizing will help stock value

NOTE: Consider the total costs of downsizing. You save salaries, but you expend extras (extra unemployment costs, severance/vacation pay, extended health/ medical benefits, outplacement expenses, fattening the retirement pot) and risk revenues (when you cut sales reps in the field, who will field your sales leads?).

BOTTOMLINE: Personnel and budgetary cuts should be deep—but not too deep. People are the lifeblood of any company. Make the cuts too drastic and the company might bleed to death.

PROGRAM PLANNING SUMMARY

All the program planning in the world is useless unless you plan to do something with it. Now that you have a general feel for generic issues, you need to spar with the specifics.

The questions are short and sweet. Don't feel bitter about having to address them.

1. When are we going to lay people off?

2. When are we going to tell them (keeping in mind any relevant legislative mandates)?

3. When should we/must we notify others (state/local offices, media, etc.)?

4. What downsizing option(s) are we going to use?

5. What are the implementation specifics of the plan (e.g., are we offering one week of severance pay for every year worked or two?)?

6. Who qualifies for outplacement assistance?

7. Who provides which outplacement services?

8. How many employees are going to lose their jobs?

9. What are the budgetary goals of the downsizing program?

10. Who will lose their jobs? Attach a list of names.

P A R T

IV

Implementation

WATCH OUT FOR PITFALLS
AS YOU PREPARE TO IMPLEMENT!

IMPLEMENTATION INTRODUCTION

The key to successful implementation (pages 49 to 61) is program planning (pages 21 to 48).

If you skipped the analytical appetizers to get to the meat of the matter, there is a culinary caveat that needs to be served:

> *Implementation without structure—without the proper preplanning—is distraction, not action. Avoiding the preliminaries voids your best chance for success.*

That said, the implementation phase of downsizing delivers dilemmas of its own. The major problems include:

☑ Announcing the Action

☑ Continuing Communications

☑ Stabilizing the Staff

☑ Creating Contentment among Constituents

The checklists on the following pages will help you supplant these perennial problems.

ANNOUNCING THE ACTION

"DIM-PLEMENTATION"

According to Fortune magazine, "When BHP Petroleum was cutting back its oil and gas operations in Houston a couple of years ago, the company called a meeting of the entire staff. Each employee was given an envelope with A or B written on it. Then the B's were sent to another room—and told they were being laid off. 'A mass firing is always humiliating and dehumanizing,' says a Houston headhunter who helped some of the refugees find new jobs. Have the courtesy—and the guts—to lay people off in private, one by one."

AN ENLIGHTENED APPROACH

1. Always handle terminations one-on-one (manager to individual employee).

2. If this seems too difficult logistically, refer back to point #1 (if you can *hire* individually you can *fire* individually).

3. Terminations should be firm, clear and unambiguous.

4. The message should be honest and consistent.

5. Be apologetic about the need to downsize, not the downsizing itself.

6. Emphasize the collective origin/impact of the problem which precipitated the downsizing.

7. Immediately following the layoff announcement, give the employee all available information (termination date, outplacement services, severance pay, extended medical benefits, availability and value of unemployment benefits, etc.).

8. Give this information in writing.

9. Customize the information ("You have ____ weeks of severance pay, ____ days of paid vacation, etc.").

10. Top management must be visible during the downsizing (e.g., make the formal announcements).

11. Anticipate and prepare for negative reactions.

12. Encourage feedback/questions.

13. Avoid confrontations and adversarial approaches.

14. Demonstrate sympathy and empathy.

15. Don't insult employees ("We just got rid of some deadwood").

16. Be sensitive to timing (one shouldn't downsize immediately after giving big raises to top management).

In short, treat employee casualties with more than casual concern. Treat them the way you would want to be treated.

TRUST ME. IT'LL WORK!

CONTINUING COMMUNICATIONS

"DIM-PLEMENTATION"

According to Personnel magazine, "One large company decided to cut costs by discontinuing the technical professionals' use of company cars. A few weeks later, top management decided to lay off approximately 15% of the employees. Although the decision to cut the cars preceded the decision to cut the people, the former decision was implemented *after* the latter one. Unfortunately, no one besides top management knew this, and some employees consequently thought that people had been cut before perks."

AN ENLIGHTENED APPROACH

There are only three priority points to practice:

1. Communicate!

2. Communicate!

3. Communicate!

Sure, you should maintain a positive tone and use appropriate humor. You need to be open and honest. The timing has to be right. The right people—top management—have to do the talking *and* the listening.

But the crucial communication component is simply to *do it*. If you continuously tell people what has happened, what is happening now, and what is going to happen, they feel like part of the team rather than apart from the team.

Where communication is concerned, the road to a healthy company is paved with good intentions. Intentionally.

STABILIZING THE STAFF

"DIM-PLEMENTATION"

According to Fortune magazine, when Arco "cut its workforce by 6,000 a few summers ago, nobody at headquarters mentioned to any of the most-valued managers that there might be good reasons to hang tight. As a result, when generous severance deals were offered all around, several stars took the package and ran. 'Their startling departures,' says a manager who is still there, 'caused an awful lot of extra drain and strain' at an already grim-enough moment."

AN ENLIGHTENED APPROACH

1. Address the downsizing
   - Remind the "survivors" that they were chosen to stay
   - Acknowledge the pain of the paring process and the need to mourn
   - Emphasize that downsizing makes the future more secure for the company and its crew
   - Stress that the downsizing is over
   - Encourage feelings of relief (it's OK not to feel guilty about other people losing their jobs)

2. Manage the change (translation: manage to make it work!)
   - Prepare employees for change
   - Make the changes beneficial to workers
   - Stress new opportunities for everyone
   - Understand employee work values
   - Restructure positions, jettison job junk (e.g., redundant or meaningless functions, oppressive procedures, etc.)
   - Clarify and verify new performance standards
   - Use buffers when needed (temp, overtime, subcontractors, outside vendors, rent out employees/their services, etc.)
   - Don't forget the little things (e.g., if you neglect scheduled employee appraisals, if the carpet starts to look ratty, etc., employees will think that corporate survival is "iffy")

IMPLEMENTATION—STABILIZING THE STAFF—(Continued)

AN ENLIGHTENED APPROACH

3. Empower employees
   - Provide additional training (managerial, teambuilding, stress management, skills, etc.)
   - Create skill ready employees through cross-training, job flexibility, cross-utilization, work rule revisions, job reclassifications, broad job assignments, new union contracts, etc.
   - Be a director, not a dictator
   - Spend some of the savings on exciting, positive programs (Time Inc. used 5% of its downsizing savings to start a new magazine)
   - Weave accountability, responsibility and authority together
   - Use participatory management
   - Help employees grow (e.g., through more versatile or more rewarding jobs)
   - Give meaningful performance evaluations
   - Provide employees with the tools (money, support staff, etc.) they need to get the job done
   - Recognize new job perceptions
   - Create a sense or purpose
   - Nourish in-house talent
   - Build alternate career paths (success isn't synonymous with supervisor)
   - Demonstrate that you value employee expertise
   - Help rebuild relationships (for example, if the contact person in a department is clipped, a replacement will need to be groomed)
   - Encourage career self-management
   - Stress the notion that security comes not from what you *do* but from what you *are* (skills, abilities, attitude, etc.)
   - Encourage employees to ask ''In what ways might I...''
   - Improve the mediating structure
   - Encourage risk-taking (even as you discourage politicizing)
   - Solicit employee suggestions
   - Stress that loyalty to the company really means loyalty to the value/contributions the company makes to society

4. Preparing for the long term

- Emphasize the need to move on
- Prioritize
- Stress long term goals
- Clarify business issues
- Compare expectations (employees, middle management, top management)
- View employees as a competitive weapon
- Integrate employees as part of the organizational strategy
- Work to rebuild confidence/trust/support
- Stay the course (don't stray the course and quickly rehire those fired)

Employee stabilization should be your major concern in downsizing. Without a stable work force, your company is a work farce. Employee stability creates corporate viability.

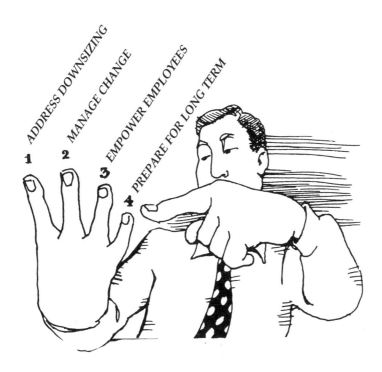

CREATING CONTENTMENT AMONG CONSTITUENTS

"DIM-PLEMENTATION"

Quoting Fortune magazine, "AT&T top management began a series of [downsizing] missteps by confiding to Wall Street security analysts that the company was planning massive job cuts. The analysts, always a gabby group, put the word out, and many AT&T employees read all about it in the newspapers before their bosses had a chance to fill them in. That brought business to a screeching half for weeks, while people speculated about what was coming next. Amid the uncertainty, at least two middle managers killed themselves."

AN ENLIGHTENED APPROACH

There are ten MIA's—Men/Women Influenced by the Action—in a corporate downsizing.

- Managers
- Laid off employees
- Survivors
- Minority workers
- Customers
- Competitors
- Suppliers
- Local community
- Media
- Shareholders

When managing MIA's, many downsizing companies focus on damage control—no, check that—they focus on *damage*. The stockholders will be upset (our stock will go down). Competitors will convince people that they need a more stable source of supply (sales will drop). Vendors will tender notices of credit cancellation (expect an outward cash flow flood).

This approach exacerbates, rather than mitigates, downsizing damage. It is a purely passive policy. Other people (and their reactions) get to call the shots while you play a defensive game—reacting to, rather than circumventing, the scenario.

''Damage control'' is the right phrase with the wrong emphasis. The weighty word is *control*. Control reactions and actions. Control the situation.

For example:

> Write a personalized letter to customers. Stress that the downsizing will not affect product/service quality, production and delivery schedules, client support services, etc. Discuss why/how you can make this claim. Expect clients to trust you based on facts, not faith.

> Emphasize that the downsizing will make your company a stronger more competitive supplier. Note that the changes being made (a more flexible production crew, less paperwork, lower production costs, etc.) benefit the buyer. Announce current plans and long term strategies to build confidence.

> In short, don't let the suppliers draw their own conclusions. Send them a picture.

IMPLEMENTATION—CREATING COMMITMENT AMONG CONTITUENTS (Continued)

AN ENLIGHTENED APPROACH

Other controlling concepts include:

- Start with secrecy. Don't let anybody leak the news before you're ready to speak the news. This means limiting the downsizing dialog to a few managers, typing your own downsizing documents to avoid secretarial sabotage, etc.

- Study security. If you think disgruntled employees may vandalize or scandalize, organize additional security forces. Crimes against property, people and corporate popularity are prevalent.

- Share the data and the decision-making process. Show people why you had to downsize and they'll show you more respect.

- Schedule constituent communications. For example, inform employees before you mess with the media, mention mandates to managers before menials, etc.

- Don't play one constituency off against another. For example, never tell stockholders that you ''got rid of deadwood'' while telling employees that you've ''got to cut expenses.''

- Refuse to buy into adversarial angles. This isn't company vs. community or business vs. blue collars. This is you doing what needs to be done to keep the company alive.

- Don't be coy. For example, when you're ready to downsize, don't hint. Announce. When you do things halfway, you are giving away 50% of the control.

> Dealing with MIA's is simple. Don't just play the downsizing game. *Run* the downsizing game. Take charge and take control. The odds are always with the house.

SUMMARY

Throughout the implementation phase, we've seen variations on a familiar theme. That is:

Control is crucial to successful program implementation

For example:

- When you announce the action you control the situation by anticipating problems and providing answers.

- You control communications by continuing them. The gossip grapevine withers in an environment of openness.

- You stabilize the workforce by controlling/extolling the present and future.

- You control constituents by being a source of information and leadership, not a source of irritation.

Control may be continuing corporate cause celebre, but that's because it often separates success from failure. You must control your downsizing destiny.

P A R T

V

Followup

FOLLOWUP

There's an old medical maxim: the operation was a success but the patient died.

This saying really speaks to the difficult downsizing diagnosis. That's why managerial MD's must continue to take the company pulse. This requires a two part operation.

OPERATION #1—EXPLORATORY SURGERY

Cut confusion. Conduct exploratory surveys. Check the following vital signs for any negative symptoms. Have their been major changes in:

- Employee morale
- Turnover
- Productivity
- Absenteeism
- Tardiness
- Stress levels in managers
- Stress levels in non-managers
- Processing/production times
- Number of departmental problems
- Number of complaints/grievances
- Expense levels
- Employee participation
- Attendance at company functions
- Number of customer complaints
- Aggregate/individual sales
- Working hours
- Communication difficulties
- Risk taking (at all levels)
- Politicking
- Individual invisibility (employees who try to stay as inconspicuous as possible)

Ask questions! You must determine if these downsizing symptoms are a temporary malady or a terminal mess.

FOLLOWUP (Continued)

OPERATION #2—VACCINATIONS

Practice preventative medicine. To vaccinate against business bloat:

1. Make it hard for people to get hired
Insure that potential personnel conform to the corporate culture. Consider using temps, outside consultants, part-timers, overtime, etc., to relieve short term needs. In short, needing help isn't synonymous with hiring help.

2. Get rid of goof-offs
Put bite into your performance reviews. When appropriate, have personnel rated by their managers, internal customers, subordinates, and peers. Measure the quantitative and the qualitative. When people aren't working out for you they shouldn't be working for you.

3. Derail the career fast track
Substitute horizontal movement for vertical lift. Refuse to promote people to staff positions until they have a broad range of line experience. Make employees pay their dues, only give promotions in due course.

4. Reward the reasonable
Reward managers for superior performance, not subordinate numbers. Focus attention on departmental profitability, not departmental population. Don't appropriate power or prestige according to personnel. In short, don't provide incentives to overstaff.

The best problem is one you avoid. Keep the company lean and mean. Then you won't have to pare down or tear down.

P A R T

VI

Case Studies

REPLACE DOWNSIZING FEARS WITH CHEERS

The proper program can turn negative notions into positive perspectives. Consider what happened when Bank of America was threatened (by First Interstate) with a hostile takeover and down-the-line downsizing.

"According to Bob Beck, Vice-President and Head of Human Resources at Bank of America, the hostile threat was ironically 'the best thing that could have happened' to the company. Tom Clawsen, Bank of America's new Chief Executive Officer saw it as an opportunity to create a powerful binding force among his discouraged employees. He announced the First Interstate Bank "FIB" Busters campaign, a move that turned employee attention away from internal struggles toward an external 'common enemy.' A week before First Interstate's bid was withdrawn, Beck said 'I hope they [First Interstate] don't give up for another month or so. This is having an extremely positive effect on our people.'"*

In short, what you see—or choose to see!—is what you get. So why not see things in a positive light?

*Source: *Personnel*, December 1987

IN SEARCH OF SURVIVORS

It isn't easy, deciding who should stay and who should be sent away. This is particularly true when you've decided to downsize based on employees' skill or productivity level.

Still, some managers manage to do it very well. Philip Spertus, Chairman and CEO of Chicago-based Intercraft Industries Corporation has a four point plan that points out the corporate keepers.

The Spertus Specifications

1. Meet with company managers. Explain the new direction and action orientation of the company. Meetings should be short and issue-oriented.

2. Discuss individual performances with middle managers ("What are you working on? What important thing should I know about? What would you do if you were me?"). Develop a rapport.

3. STEP 3 IS KEY. ASK MANAGERS "WHO ARE SOME OF THE REALLY PRODUCTIVE PEOPLE IN THE COMPANY?" You'll find that certain names reoccur with water-torture tenacity. These oft-mentioned employees are the prize.

4. Build—or rebuild!—the company around these productive people.

NOTE: This approach has a positive pathos. You are asking managers to spotlight winners, not blacken reputations. It focuses on the effective, not the defective.

It also helped Intercraft cut its headquarters staff from 85 to 35 in less than six months. Total productivity is higher; payroll costs, space costs, travel expenses, etc., are all lower.

Spertus's plan doesn't just identify winners. It helps create them!

CONTENT CONSTITUENTS

This is a business maze beaten by an amazing company: San Francisco-based Amfac Inc.

Amfac purchased Fisher (a small cheese manufacturer) from Borden. One of two plants was closed. This project had the makings of a media mess. For example:

- The plant employed approximately 400 people in the small town of Wapakoneta (population: 8500).

- Because of industry vulnerability and seller sensitivity, there was no advance layoff notice.

- Many of the employees had never worked anywhere else.

Media and image-wise, things weren't looking good.

How did Amfac maintain its positive image and mitigate a potential media mess?

Harry Matte, Sr. Vice President of Corporate Communications for Amfac, Inc., recognized a VIP (Very Important Point). You don't work around the media. You work with it.

THE AMFAC SOLUTION

According to Matte,

"Our goal was to blunt the negative impact of the news, emphasize the support Amfac was providing employees and make sure that stories appearing in print and heard over the air were accurate.

"To accomplish this, while our employees were hearing the negative news, personal visits and phone calls were being made to newspapers in Wapakoneta and five other communities within a 20-mile radius of the plant.

"We also briefed the Associated Press and United Press International bureaus in Columbus to make sure the Fisher stories that moved throughout Ohio and the region were accurate. An immediate goal was to get the complete story in that evening's news coverage. Media kits with a news release, fact sheet and backgrounders on outplacement and termination benefits were distributed. An Amfac spokesman stood by to place and respond to phone calls from reporters.

"Although newspapers which required more lead time were briefed beginning at 9 a.m., radio station contacts were delayed so that workers would be able to report the news to their families before they heard it over the radio, an important medium in the largely rural area.

"Although a negative story, the news coverage that evening was balanced. Amfac's concern and program of assistance was included in all reports—which was important to build confidence and support among workers, their families and the community." (Source: *Personnel Administrator*, January 1988).

Ohio state government applauded Amfac's handling of the downsizing. "They (Amfac) are truly setting a tone of leadership," Lt. Governor Paul Leonard said. "Let this project serve as an example of what a vacating company should do for its former home."

NOTE: This particular problem no longer exists, thanks to WARN legislation.

FOR WHOM THE BELL TOLLS

This is an example of "seventh heaven"; that is, an example of how a company can use the seventh downsizing option—terminating an entire job position/level—to trim staff while expanding employee opportunities.

Pacific Bell expects to downsize approximately 11,000 employees over a five year period. The company periodically (twice a year) forecasts what will cause specific reductions/increases in particular positions. Forecasts (which predict how new technology, attrition, trends, etc., are expected to impact specific job titles) *are passed on to employees*. Employees can then retrain and aim for those jobs with the rosiest future forecast.

NOTE: The forecasts (for sample pages, see pages 74–75) are guidelines, not guarantees. Pacific Bell doesn't guarantee a given number of specific jobs or who would get them. But the foresight of a well reasoned forecast is as close to 20/20 career eyesight as an employee can get.

Pacific Bell has received, and deserves to receive, prolific praise for its downsizing approach. In an uncertain world, this is certainly an exemplary way to treat employees.

PAC BELL EXAMPLE NEXT PAGE

PAC BELL EXHIBIT

Introduction

This forecast and related data displayed on the following pages is the result of the combined effort of the Communications Workers of American and Pacific Bell/Nevada Bell. Data collection is from all officer entities.

The following pages communicate information regarding job opportunities, surplus jobs, and basic job skills. The Governance Board's expectations are that non-salaried employees can utilize this information to determine:

- when and why their job is being eliminated, moved, consolidated, functionalized, etc.
- what jobs will be available in the future and where they might be.
- what basic job skills are required to perform current and future jobs.
- what career development resources are available to help employees successfully move to new jobs.

The forecast may not always accurately predict what actually will happen to your job, but the forecast (and it is only a forecast, not a commitment or a business plan), represents the best information we have available at the time of its publication. Forecasts will be published twice each year.

TECHNOLOGICAL CHANGE (ETC.)			
Northern California - *Continued*			
PROJECT	**LOCATION**	**IMPLEMENT DATE**	**FORCE IMPACT**
TECH ACCESS **Special Services** (Continued)	Bakersfield	3rd Quarter 90	
TECH ACCESS **Maintenance** (Field access to mechanized support systems)	Coast	1st Quarter 90	
	Sierra	1st Quarter 90	
	Monticello	1st Quarter 90	
AABS (Automated Alternate Billing System)	Sacramento	3rd Quarter 91	
Consolidation of Center (Data Maintenance Group and Mini-computer Maintenance Group)	Sacramento J. Street	1st Quarter 90	

Work Force Trends - 1992

Sector - Southern California

	Force As of Sept 89	Attrition[1]	Projected[2] Opportunities Thru 12/92	Projected[3] Surplus Thru 12/92	Trend[4] 1989-1992
Analyst					
Building Mechanic					
Building Specialist					
Cashier					
Central Office Associate					
Collector					
Communications Technician					
Communications Technician (ESS)					
Communications Technician (Toll)					
Computer Operator					
Copy Service Artist					
Customer Associate					
Data/Engineering Administrator					
Data Entry Associate					
Data Specialist					
Engineering Assistant					
Equipment Specialist					
Facilities/Assignment Admin.					
Facilities Technician					
FACS Administrator					
Maintenance Administrator					
Medical Assistant					
Messenger (Motorized)					
Office Associate					
Operations Administrator					
Operator					
Outside Plant Technician					
Reports/Staff Associate					
Service Assistant					
Service Representative					
Services Technician					
Splicing Technician					
Supply Service Attendant					

P A R T

VII

Summary

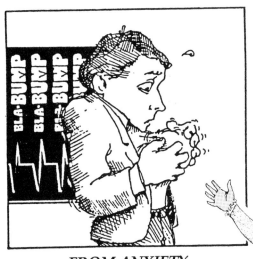

FROM ANXIETY

TO SUCCESS

SUMMARY

By now, you've probably replaced your downsizing trepidation with an uplifting revelation:

Successful downsizing doesn't require miracles.
It only requires *basic management*.

Look again at the basic components of downsizing and you'll see the light.

Strategic Planning

Strategic planning is crucial, whether you're getting ahead or getting cut back. Successful companies continuously analyze where they are and where they want to be. The difference between downsizing plans and general down-the-road plans is a simple one. Downsizing plans are imminent and usable, the more futuristic fabrications are eminent and muse-able.

Program Planning

Issues of who, what, when, why and how are not limited to downsizing. They are common to all corporate calculations. Deciding on a downsizing option, for example, is no different than pragmatically picking a new product. Managers weight the pros and cons before making the heavy decision.

Implementation

Implementation isn't a foreign concept either. Implementation is what you do every day from 8 to 5. You make things—plans—happen. Downsizing plans may be less popular then upscaling plans, but when you get down to it implementation is universal.

Followup

In business, followup is a "must-have"—not a "must have thought about doing it a million times." Without followup, successful businesses can't judge their success. Without followup, companies can't take their internal pulse. Without followup, downsizing companies find themselves with serious new problems.

Remember our original premise and promise: forget downsizing doom and gloom. Downsizing can be an uplifting experience, both for corporate profits and your own managerial career. Cutbacks offer perils *and* payoffs. Decide to treat the situation as a gain rather than a strain. Your downsizing success is up to you.

NOTES

FOR OTHER FIFTY-MINUTE SELF-STUDY BOOKS
SEE ORDER FORM AT THE BACK OF THE BOOK.

NOTES

FOR OTHER FIFTY-MINUTE SELF-STUDY BOOKS
SEE ORDER FORM AT THE BACK OF THE BOOK.

NOTES

FOR OTHER FIFTY-MINUTE SELF-STUDY BOOKS
SEE ORDER FORM AT THE BACK OF THE BOOK.

NOTES

NOTES

ORDER FORM
THE FIFTY-MINUTE SERIES

Quantity	Title	Code #	Price	Amount
	MANAGEMENT TRAINING			
	Self-Managing Teams	00-0	$7.95	
	Delegating for Results	008-6	$7.95	
	Successful Negotiation — Revised	09-2	$7.95	
	Increasing Employee Productivity	10-8	$7.95	
	Personal Performance Contracts — Revised	12-2	$7.95	
	Team Building — Revised	16-5	$7.95	
	Effective Meeting Skills	33-5	$7.95	
	An Honest Day's Work: Motivating Employees	39-4	$7.95	
	Managing Disagreement Constructively	41-6	$7.95	
	Learning To Lead	43-4	$7.95	
	The Fifty-Minute Supervisor — 2/e	58-0	$7.95	
	Leadership Skills for Women	62-9	$7.95	
	Coaching & Counseling	68-8	$7.95	
	Ethics in Business	69-6	$7.95	
	Understanding Organizational Change	71-8	$7.95	
	Project Management	75-0	$7.95	
	Risk Taking	076-9	$7.95	
	Managing Organizational Change	80-7	$7.95	
	Working Together in a Multi-Cultural Organization	85-8	$7.95	
	Selecting And Working With Consultants	87-4	$7.95	
	Empowerment	096-5	$7.95	
	Managing for Commitment	099-X	$7.95	
	Rate Your Skills as a Manager	101-5	$7.95	
	PERSONNEL/HUMAN RESOURCES			
	Your First Thirty Days: A Professional Image in a New Job	003-5	$7.95	
	Office Management: A Guide to Productivity	005-1	$7.95	
	Men and Women: Partners at Work	009-4	$7.95	
	Effective Performance Appraisals — Revised	11-4	$7.95	
	Quality Interviewing — Revised	13-0	$7.95	
	Personal Counseling	14-9	$7.95	
	Giving and Receiving Criticism	023-X	$7.95	
	Attacking Absenteeism	042-6	$7.95	
	New Employee Orientation	46-7	$7.95	
	Professional Excellence for Secretaries	52-1	$7.95	
	Guide to Affirmative Action	54-8	$7.95	
	Writing a Human Resources Manual	70-X	$7.95	
	Downsizing Without Disaster	081-7	$7.95	
	Winning at Human Relations	86-6	$7.95	
	High Performance Hiring	088-4	$7.95	
	COMMUNICATIONS			
	Technical Writing in the Corporate World	004-3	$7.95	
	Effective Presentation Skills	24-6	$7.95	
	Better Business Writing — Revised	25-4	$7.95	

Quantity	Title	Code #	Price	Amount
	COMMUNICATIONS (continued)			
	The Business of Listening	34-3	$7.95	
	Writing Fitness	35-1	$7.95	
	The Art of Communicating	45-9	$7.95	
	Technical Presentation Skills	55-6	$7.95	
	Making Humor Work	61-0	$7.95	
	50 One Minute Tips to Better Communication	071-X	$7.95	
	Speed-Reading in Business	78-5	$7.95	
	Influencing Others	84-X	$7.95	
	PERSONAL IMPROVEMENT			
	Attitude: Your Most Priceless Possession — Revised	011-6	$7.95	
	Personal Time Management	22-X	$7.95	
	Successful Self-Management	26-2	$7.95	
	Business Etiquette And Professionalism	32-9	$7.95	
	Balancing Home & Career — Revised	35-3	$7.95	
	Developing Positive Assertiveness	38-6	$7.95	
	The Telephone and Time Management	53-X	$7.95	
	Memory Skills in Business	56-4	$7.95	
	Developing Self-Esteem	66-1	$7.95	
	Managing Personal Change	74-2	$7.95	
	Finding Your Purpose	072-8	$7.95	
	Concentration!	073-6	$7.95	
	Plan Your Work/Work Your Plan!	078-7	$7.95	
	Stop Procrastinating: Get To Work!	88-2	$7.95	
	12 Steps to Self-Improvement	102-3	$7.95	
	CREATIVITY			
	Systematic Problem Solving & Decision Making	63-7	$7.95	
	Creativity in Business	67-X	$7.95	
	Intuitive Decision Making	098-1	$7.95	
	TRAINING			
	Training Managers to Train	43-2	$7.95	
	Visual Aids in Business	77-7	$7.95	
	Developing Instructional Design	076-0	$7.95	
	Training Methods That Work	082-5	$7.95	
	WELLNESS			
	Mental Fitness: A Guide to Emotional Health	15-7	$7.95	
	Wellness in the Workplace	020-5	$7.95	
	Personal Wellness	21-3	$7.95	
	Preventing Job Burnout	23-8	$7.95	
	Job Performance and Chemical Dependency	27-0	$7.95	
	Overcoming Anxiety	29-9	$7.95	
	Productivity at the Workstation	41-8	$7.95	
	Healthy Strategies for Working Women	079-5	$7.95	
	CUSTOMER SERVICE/SALES TRAINING			
	Sales Training Basics — Revised	02-5	$7.95	
	Restaurant Server's Guide — Revised	08-4	$7.95	
	Effective Sales Management	31-0	$7.95	

Quantity	Title	Code #	Price	Amount
	CUSTOMER SERVICE/SALES TRAINING (continued)			
	Professional Selling	42-4	$7.95	
	Telemarketing Basics	60-2	$7.95	
	Telephone Courtesy & Customer Service — Revised	64-7	$7.95	
	Calming Upset Customers	65-3	$7.95	
	Quality at Work	72-6	$7.95	
	Managing Quality Customer Service	83-1	$7.95	
	Customer Satisfaction — Revised	84-1	$7.95	
	Quality Customer Service — Revised	95-5	$7.95	
	SMALL BUSINESS/FINANCIAL PLANNING			
	Consulting for Success	006-X	$7.95	
	Understanding Financial Statements	22-1	$7.95	
	Marketing Your Consulting or Professional Services	40-8	$7.95	
	Starting Your New Business	44-0	$7.95	
	Direct Mail Magic	075-2	$7.95	
	Credits & Collections	080-9	$7.95	
	Publicity Power	82-3	$7.95	
	Writing & Implementing Your Marketing Plan	083-3	$7.95	
	Personal Financial Fitness — Revised	89-0	$7.95	
	Financial Planning With Employee Benefits	90-4	$7.95	
	ADULT LITERACY/BASIC LEARNING			
	Returning to Learning: Getting Your G.E.D.	02-7	$7.95	
	Study Skills Strategies — Revised	05-X	$7.95	
	The College Experience	07-8	$7.95	
	Basic Business Math	24-8	$7.95	
	Becoming an Effective Tutor	28-0	$7.95	
	Reading Improvement	086-8	$7.95	
	Introduction to Microcomputers	087-6	$7.95	
	Clear Writing	094-9	$7.95	
	Building Blocks of Business Writing	095-7	$7.95	
	Language, Customs & Protocol	097-3	$7.95	
	CAREER BUILDING			
	Career Discovery	07-6	$7.95	
	Effective Networking	30-2	$7.95	
	Preparing for Your Interview	33-7	$7.95	
	Plan B: Protecting Your Career	48-3	$7.95	
	I Got The Job!	59-9	$7.95	
	Job Search That Works	105-8	$7.95	

NOTE: ORDERS TOTALING LESS THAN $25.00 MUST BE PREPAID

	Amount
Total Books	
Less Discount	
Total	
California Tax (California residents add 7%)	
Shipping	
TOTAL	

☐ Please send me a free Video Catalog.   ☐ Please add my name to your mailing list.

 ☐ Mastercard   **VISA** ☐ VISA   ☐ AMEX   Exp. Date _____

Account No. _____   Name (as appears on card) _____

Ship to: _____   Bill to: _____

_____   _____

_____   _____

_____   _____

Phone number: _____   P.O. #: _____

All orders of less than $25.00 must be prepaid. Bill to orders require a company P.O.#. For more information, call (415) 949-4888 or FAX (415) 949-1610.